TOP TRUMPS®
EXTREME
WHEELS 2

This book is officially licensed by Winning Moves UK Ltd,
owners of the Top Trumps registered trademark.

Richard Dredge has asserted his right to be identified as the
author of this book.

First published in January 2009

British Library Cataloguing-in-Publication Data:
A catalogue record for this book is available from the British Library

ISBN 978 1 84425 691 4

Library of Congress catalog card no. 2008939590

Published by Haynes Publishing,
Sparkford, Yeovil, Somerset BA22 7JJ, UK
Tel: 01963 442030 Fax: 01963 440001
Int. tel: +44 1963 442030 Int. fax: +44 1963 440001
Email: sales@haynes.co.uk
Website: www.haynes.co.uk

Haynes North America, Inc.,
861 Lawrence Drive, Newbury Park, California 91320, USA

Printed and bound in Great Britain by J. H. Haynes & Co. Ltd, Sparkford

Photographic credits: all photographs sourced from
www.magiccarpics.co.uk unless stated otherwise.

The Author

Richard Dredge got addicted to cars when he was a child, rebuilding his
first Triumph at 16. He contributes to publications such as *Octane*, *Practical
Classics* and *Auto Express*. For a fuller CV, look at www.richarddredge.com

TOP TRUMPS®

EXTREME WHEELS 2

Contents

About
Top Trumps

It's now more than 30 years since Britain's kids first caught the Top Trumps craze. The game remained hugely popular until the 1990s, when it slowly drifted into obscurity. Then, in 1999, UK games company Winning Moves discovered it, bought it, dusted it down, gave it a thorough makeover and introduced it to a whole new generation. And so the Top Trumps legend continues.

Nowadays, there are Top Trumps titles for just about everyone, with subjects about animals, cars, ships, aircraft and all the great films and TV shows. Top Trumps is now even more popular than before. In Britain, a pack of Top Trumps is bought every six seconds! And it's not just British children who love the game. Children in Australasia, the Far East, the Middle East, all over Europe and in North America can buy Top Trumps at their local shops.

Today you can even play the game on the internet, interactive DVD, your games console and even your mobile phone.

You've played the game...

Now read the book!

Haynes Publishing and Top Trumps have teamed up to bring you this exciting new Top Trumps book, in which you will find even more pictures, details and statistics.

Top Trumps: Extreme Wheels 2 features another 45 of the world's fastest, most innovative, futuristic or wacky vehicles, from the lairy FAB Design S60 BT to the stunning Mazda Taiki and the incredible Rinspeed sQuba. Packed with fascinating facts, stunning photographs and all the vital statistics, this is the essential pocket guide.

Look out for other Top Trumps books from Haynes Publishing – even more facts, even more fun!

AC Schnitzer
Tension

AC Schnitzer
Tension

You can't accuse the standard BMW M6 of having no presence, but by the time AC Schnitzer had got its hands on the car and created the Tension concept, it had cranked up the aesthetics to 12. With a mixture of black and bright orange paintwork, plus chromed 20-inch wheels and added detailing, the Tension was definitely striking. However, when it came to offering the car for sale, things were toned down a bit – but not much! Not only is the paintwork more sober, but the conversion can be based on the more lowly 630i, 645Ci or 650i. Buyers can opt for tweaks to the standard powerplant or a full-on 5.1-litre V8 transplant. In this latter form there's a hefty 411bhp on tap, which is enough to take the car to around 180mph.

Statistics

Type of vehicle	**Grand Tourer**
Year	**2006**
Country of origin	**Germany**
Length	**4820mm**
Width	**1855mm**
Height	**1374mm**
Engine size	**5.1 litres**
Engine type	**Front-mounted petrol V8**
Max power	**411bhp**
Max speed	**180mph**
Number of seats	**4**
Special features	**Presence, thanks to a ridiculously lairy paint job and massive chromed alloy wheels**
Extreme rating	**7**

Andy Carter
Top Fuel Dragster

Andy Carter
Top Fuel Dragster

Cars come no more extreme than a top fuel dragster. Built for one reason only – to accelerate as quickly as possible – these cars represent the pinnacle of automotive engineering. Capable of accelerating from a standstill to around 200mph in just six seconds or so over a 440-yard stretch of Tarmac, a top fuel dragster gathers speed faster than a jumbo jet, a fighter jet, or a Formula One race car. Each cylinder produces around 1000bhp, and with a 0–100mph time of under a second, a top fuel dragster leaves the start line with a force nearly five times that of gravity, the same force of the space shuttle when it leaves the launch pad at Cape Canaveral. But it all comes at a cost: these monsters consume 4–5 gallons of fuel during a quarter-mile run, equivalent to 16–20 gallons per mile!

Statistics

Type of vehicle	**Dragster**
Year	**2006**
Country of origin	**USA**
Length	**7600mm**
Width	**1200mm**
Height	**2300mm**
Engine size	**8190cc**
Engine type	**Rear-mounted supercharged nitromethane V8**
Max power	**8000bhp**
Max speed	**317mph**
Number of seats	**1**
Special features	**A crippling thirst plus unfeasible levels of acceleration**
Extreme rating	**10**

Pictures courtesy of www.andycarter.net

Aptera
Typ-1

Aptera
Typ-1

Taking its name from the Greek for 'wingless flight', the Aptera is a cross between an aeroplane and a car. Amazingly aerodynamic, the brains behind the project is Steve Fambro, who set out to create a passenger vehicle that is safe, comfortable and more fuel-efficient than anything ever produced. Following an intensive study of aerodynamics and composite aircraft construction, this low-drag, aerodynamic body shape was achieved without sacrificing comfort, drivability or safety – although only a pair of adults plus one child can be comfortably accommodated. Designed from the ground up as an electric vehicle, the Aptera is offered in pure electric or petrol/electric hybrid guises, although it's offered only in California, which is also where the cars are built.

Statistics

Type of vehicle	Electric commuter car
Year	2008
Country of origin	USA
Length	N/A
Width	N/A
Height	N/A
Engine size	N/A
Engine type	Plug-in hybrid (three-phase electric motor +
Max power	N/A
Max speed	85mph
Number of seats	2+1
Special features	Amazing shape, brilliant aerodynamics, clever technology
Extreme rating	10

ASI
Tetsu GTR

ASI
Tetsu GTR

There was a time when a Bentley was not only sacred territory – so tuners went nowhere near them – but the cars were so incredibly exclusive that aftermarket modifications were unnecessary. After all, why make your Bentley stand out when there were no others around? The Continental GT changed that, with so many being made each year, that there's now one on every street corner. That's why companies such as ASI sprang up to offer crazy bodywork conversions, mad colour schemes and bare carbon-fibre panelling to produce a more high-tech look. And for those who feel that 600bhp is a bit lame, ASI can also offer engine upgrades such as free-flowing exhausts, ECU tweaks and enlarged turbocharger turbines to produce up to 800bhp.

Statistics

Type of vehicle	Grand tourer
Year	2008
Country of origin	England/Japan
Length	4804mm
Width	2070mm
Height	1390mm
Engine size	5998cc
Engine type	Front-mounted turbocharged petrol W12
Max power	800bhp
Max speed	200mph+
Number of seats	4
Special features	Naked carbon-fibre panels, crazy nose design
Extreme rating	9

Audi
Q7 V12 TDi

Audi
Q7 V12 TDi

It may not look that extreme, but delve beneath that aggressive skin and there are some truly astonishing figures associated with the Audi Q7. For example, the engine might burn diesel, but it's still got a dozen cylinders, which when working at full chat can generate a crazy 493bhp. More impressive though is the 758lb ft of torque on offer, which can catapult the Q7 to 62mph in just 4.9 seconds. Yet here's an off-roader that can transport seven adults at high speeds across continents – not that it'll be breaking any economy records in the process. Developed by the same quattro gmbh outfit that also engineered the RS4 and RS6, the Q7 is in good company – especially when you consider that the awesome powerplant in the nose was inspired by the one fitted to Audi's R10 endurance racer.

Statistics

Type of vehicle	**Seven-seater off-roader**
Year	**2008**
Country of origin	**Germany**
Length	**5086mm**
Width	**1983mm**
Height	**1737mm**
Engine size	**5934cc**
Engine type	**Front-mounted V12 turbodiesel**
Max power	**493bhp**
Max speed	**155mph**
Number of seats	**7**
Special features	**That V12 turbodiesel engine, which generates a crazy 758lb ft of torque**
Extreme rating	**6**

Avalanche Engineering
Rock Crawler

Avalanche Engineering
Rock Crawler

When Avalanche Engineering claims its Rock Crawler is an 'all terrain vehicle,' it really does mean it's capable of tackling any terrain that you throw at it. With around 14 inches of suspension travel and ridiculous levels of ground clearance, the Rock Crawler can negotiate anything from a massive boulder to a fallen tree. it helps that there's just over 500bhp on tap too; when trying to tackle the side of a cliff, mountains of torque is just the ticket – and that's just what the Rock Crawler can offer with its 565lb ft at little more than tickover. Built to withstand the harshest of environments, the Rock Crawler isn't built for comfort though; it's a stripped out monster that costs well over $60,000 if fully built by the factory.

Type of vehicle	**All-terrain vehicle**
Year	**2008**
Country of origin	**USA**
Length	**4191mm**
Width	**1600mm**
Height	**N/A**
Engine size	**8223cc**
Engine type	**Front-mounted petrol V8**
Max power	**502bhp**
Max speed	**N/A**
Number of seats	**4**
Special features	**Go-anywhere capabilities, plus 502bhp in a buggy**
Extreme rating	**10**

Boulevard Customs
Urban Whip

Boulevard Customs
Urban Whip

Few would accuse Mercedes of creating cool-looking cars, but this is what happened when the company handed over one of its GLK350s to US custom car outfit Boulevard Customs, for the 2008 SEMA modified car show at Las Vegas. Lowered by 64mm and with a 26-inch chromed alloy at each corner, the GLK has a sensational stance, which is set off by the fitment of a custom-built braking system, with 381mm discs at the front and 344mm items at the rear. The Urban Whip sounds as good as it looks too, thanks to a 5700-watt JL Audio sound system comprising eight amplifiers and six subwoofers. However, perhaps the most radical change made by Boulevard was to cut off the roof, giving the Merc a speedster look. Perhaps it'll inspire Merc's own designers to be a bit more creative, but don't bank on it.

Statistics

Type of vehicle	Open-topped SUV
Year	2008
Country of origin	Germany/USA
Length	4529mm
Width	Approx 2000mm
Height	Approx 1400mm
Engine size	3.5-litre
Engine type	Front-mounted petrol V6
Max power	286bhp
Max speed	143mph
Number of seats	4
Special features	26-inch wheels, a 5700-watt hi-fi installation
Extreme rating	9

Brabus
Bullitt Black Arrow

Brabus
Bullitt Black Arrow

How much performance would you say a junior saloon really needs? How about 130mph? Or maybe 150mph? Or do you think that 225mph, (that's a cool 360km/h), is just what the doctor ordered? That's what this crazy C-Class saloon can do after it's been through the workshops of German tuning company Brabus. At the heart of the Bullitt Black Arrow is the twin-turbo 720bhp V12 that's usually seen nestling in the engine bay of Maybach's largest saloons – yet this is the smallest saloon in the Mercedes stable! The result is a car that can sprint to 186mph from a standing start in just 24.5 seconds – and getting to 62mph takes all of 3.9 seconds. There's a catch of course; the Bullitt Black Arrow costs a whopping 348,000 euros.

Statistics

Type of vehicle	**Four-door saloon**
Year	**2008**
Country of origin	**Germany**
Length	**4590mm**
Width	**1830mm**
Height	**1402mm**
Engine size	**6233cc**
Engine type	**Twin-turbo V12 petrol**
Max power	**720bhp**
Max speed	**225mph**
Number of seats	**5**
Special features	**Insane power and performance potential through seriously impressive engineering**
Extreme rating	**8**

Callaway
C16 Speedster

Callaway
C16 Speedster

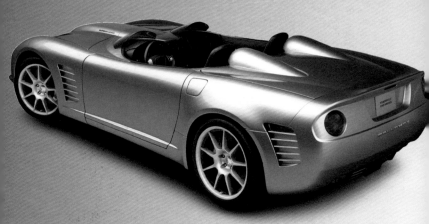

If you like your Corvettes on the spicy side, Callaway has long been happy to heat things up. As long ago as 1989 the company was building its Corvette-based Sledgehammer, which was capable of 254mph. Things have been toned down with more recent conversions of America's greatest sportscar however, as the company's C16 conversion offers a mere 650bhp and 206mph. Shrinking violets can buy the standard coupé or convertible editions, but for those who must have nothing less than the ultimate, there's this fabulous Speedster available, with aeroscreens, fairings and the most gorgeous detailing this side of a Spyker. The golden rule still applies though; if you have to ask, you can't afford it…

Statistics

Type of vehicle	**Roadster**
Year	**2006**
Country of origin	**USA**
Length	**4100mm**
Width	**1844mm**
Height	**1222mm**
Engine size	**6200cc**
Engine type	**Supercharged petrol V8**
Max power	**650bhp**
Max speed	**206mph**
Number of seats	**2**
Special features	**Fearsome power and performance combined with svelte lines**
Extreme rating	**8**

Campagna
T-Rex

Campagna
T-Rex

Lotus founder Colin Chapman had a favourite saying, which was for the ultimate in performance and agility to "just add lightness". That's the rule that Daniel Campagna stuck to when he set about creating an efficient driver's car way back in 1990, working in conjunction with some of the best engineers in the business. The T-Rex three-wheeler was the result of those efforts, the thinking being that its configuration should give it the performance and agility of a motorbike but with the stability of a car. Despite packing a mere 1352cc the T-Rex can top 140mph thanks to a 410kg kerb weight – something that also contributes greatly to an ability to sprint from a standing start to 60mph in just 4.1 seconds.

Statistics

Type of vehicle	Three-wheeled sportscar
Year	2005
Country of origin	Canada
Length	3500mm
Width	1981mm
Height	1067mm
Engine size	1352cc
Engine type	Rear-mounted petrol four-cylinder
Max power	200bhp
Max speed	140mph
Number of seats	2
Special features	Astonishing performance combined with brilliant economy
Extreme rating	8

Carver
One

Carver
One

If you're not worried about having the same wheel count as a Reliant Robin, the Carver One could be just the car for you. Sporting just three wheels, the Carver is an eco car with a difference as it can carry just two people and is powered by a tiny engine that can give up to 40mpg while also providing a top speed of around 115mph. Those figures might not sound especially impressive, but get into the driving seat and you'll be having far too much fun to care. With a bodyshell that tilts independently of the chassis that contains the running gear, the Carver can bank from left to right in under a second – ensuring that if you let rip on a twisty road, any passenger in the back is likely to feel pretty sea sick by the time they get out again.

Statistics

Type of vehicle	Three-wheeler
Year	2007
Country of origin	Holland
Length	3400mm
Width	1300mm
Height	1400mm
Engine size	659cc
Engine type	Turbocharged 4-cylinder petrol
Max power	68bhp
Max speed	115mph
Number of seats	2
Special features	A bodyshell that tilts independently of the chassis, tandem seating
Extreme rating	8

Caterham
RST

Caterham
RST

Just eight examples of the £115,000 Caterham RST were built,
all of which were sold before the first one had even come off the
production line. Packing over 300lb ft of torque and in excess of
500bhp, to give a power-to-weight ratio of around 1000bhp per ton,
the car was such an animal that anyone wanting to buy one had to
go on a two-day training course to learn how to handle the thing.
Indeed, the RST was such a beast that it was electronically limited to
150mph to stop it from taking off, while the 0-60mph sprint could be
despatched in less than three seconds, thanks to a range of complex
electronics that enabled the power to be as deployed as effectively
as possible. Caterham has produced some crazy machines before,
but it's hard to see how the company will top this one.

Statistics

Type of vehicle	Two-seater roadster
Year	2008
Country of origin	UK
Length	3530mm
Width	1685mm
Height	1140mm
Engine size	2.4 litres
Engine type	Supercharged V8 petrol
Max power	500bhp+
Max speed	150mph
Number of seats	2
Special features	Ballistic performance plus ultra-cool cosmetic updates to a classic shape
Extreme rating	7

Checker
Aerobus

MP ME RIDE
ETLY LIMOUSINES.CO
TAKING CARE OF BUSINESS
SOH 42R

Checker
Aerobus

There was a time when any New York taxi driver worth his salt
wouldn't buy anything other than a Checker cab, but the company
closed its doors in 1983 with the last example taken off New York's
streets in 1999. Those were standard four-door Checker saloons
though; what you see here is one of the ultra-rare Aerobus limousines,
77 of which were built and just 10 or so survive. Created to serve
hotels as ideal airport-run transport, for many years the Aerobus held
the world record for being the longest production car – on top of the
77 saloons there were also 3,341 estate editions made, which sold far
better thanks to the increased luggage capacity. Impressively, either
version is capable of around 100mph, but no matter how it's driven,
an Aerobus is unlikely to do much more than 8mpg. Ouch!

Statistics

Type of vehicle	**Stretch saloon**
Year	**1976**
Country of origin	**USA**
Length	**6877mm**
Width	**1930mm**
Height	**1581mm**
Engine size	**5209cc**
Engine type	**Front-mounted petrol V8**
Max power	**190bhp**
Max speed	**100mph**
Number of seats	**13**
Special features	**Eight doors, 13 seats, massive presence**
Extreme rating	**9**

Chevrolet
Newmad

Chevrolet
Newmad

One of the coolest estate cars ever created, the 1955 Chevrolet Nomad is a true design icon. However, that doesn't mean there's no room for improvement, as David Hall proved when he set out to create his own interpretaion of the theme. Wittilly renamed 'Newmad', this Chevy for the 21st century is one of the neatest hot-rods ever devised. So it should be; with over 3,000 body, chassis and interior modifications made to the original production car, the attention to detail is mind-blowing. The roof has been sectioned, the pillars chopped, the wings elongated and the lighting altered. The engine bay and cabin have received the same level of attention, but if you fancy creating something similar, bear in mind that Newmad consumed no fewer than 24,000 man hours to build, at a cost of around $1.3m. Perhaps a standard edition is cool enough after all…

Statistics

Type of vehicle	**Custom estate car**
Year	**1955**
Country of origin	**USA**
Length	**5175mm**
Width	**1880mm**
Height	**1420mm**
Engine size	**8125cc**
Engine type	**Petrol V8**
Max power	**540bhp**
Max speed	**Approx 145mph**
Number of seats	**4**
Special features	**A seriously classic style with a modern interpretation**
Extreme rating	**7**

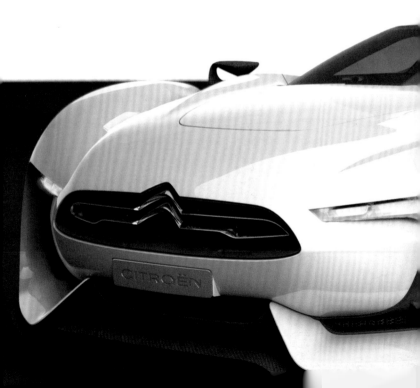

Citroen
GT

It's more usual for a supercar to be incorporated into an arcade game once it's been offered for sale for a while, but in the case of Citroen's GT concept car, it was the other way round. Inspired by one of the many supercars in the Gran Turismo 5 line up, the non-running concept made its debut at the 2008 Paris motor show. As a static prototype, the GT didn't have to be remotely practical in anyway, but the car was designed in such a way that it could be built in tiny numbers as an ultra-exclusive road car. The big hurdle though was the proposed means of motive power; a hydrogen fuel cell powering electric motors for each wheel. While such technology is still a long way off, one day it'll be an affordable production reality. Maybe!

Statistics

Type of vehicle	Supercar
Year	2008
Country of origin	France
Length	4960mm
Width	2080mm
Height	1090mm
Engine size	N/A
Engine type	Fuel cell
Max power	Non-runner
Max speed	N/A
Number of seats	2
Special features	Fuel cell propulsion, computer game-inspired, active aerodynamics, gullwing doors
Extreme rating	10

Covini
C6W

Covini
C6W

Covini claims that its C6W is the world's first six-wheeled supercar, so the company has obviously never heard of the Panther Six. Bearing in mind that just a pair of the Panthers were constructed, such an oversight is understandable – but there's little evidence that the Covini will be any more common. Powered by a 4.2-litre V8, the most striking thing about the Covini is its four front wheels, there to increase braking power as well as directional stability. Despite having to accommodate one axle more than usual, the C6W tips the scales at just 1200kg, and when this is combined with 440bhp, the top speed is claimed to be somewhere in the region of 185mph. Those horses are sent to the rear wheels only, via a six-speed sequential manual transmission.

Statistics

Type of vehicle	Supercar
Year	2005
Country of origin	Italy
Length	4180mm
Width	1990mm
Height	1080mm
Engine size	4200cc
Engine type	Rear-mounted petrol V8
Max power	440bhp
Max speed	185mph
Number of seats	2
Special features	Four wheels at the front, plus a striking exterior design
Extreme rating	9

FAB Design
S60 BT

FAB Design
S60 BT

It's a shame that Switzerland doesn't produce its own cars, because when companies such as FAB Design and Rinspeed put a car together, you can never accuse them of being dull. Focusing exclusively on uprating the cars of Mercedes-Benz, FAB Design specialises in producing some of the most far-out creations ever seen. Take the S60 for example; based on the R230 Mercedes SL600, there's nothing remotely subtle about this confection, from its pearlescent paintwork to its lairy alloys, taking in pumped-up wheelarches and beetle-wing doors along the way. While the focus is largely on applying retina-frying paintwork and dubious bodykits, customers can also indulge in a highly modified engine that pumps out up to 650bhp – enough to lower the 0–62mph dash to just 4.2 seconds. But then the standard model takes just 4.5 seconds…

Statistics

Type of vehicle	**Sportscar**
Year	**2007**
Country of origin	**Germany/ Switzerland**
Length	**4605mm**
Width	**1940mm**
Height	**1317mm**
Engine size	**5513cc**
Engine type	**Front-mounted petrol V12**
Max power	**650bhp**
Max speed	**200mph**
Number of seats	**2**
Special features	**Nauseous paint jobs, wide arches, eye-searing interiors**
Extreme rating	**8**

Ford
GT90

Ford
GT90

When Ford came up with New Edge styling, it needed something impressive to show what the theme was all about – and it would have been hard to come up with anything more extreme than the GT90, with its mass of straight edges and sharp lines. It may not have been beautiful but the GT90 was certainly dramatic – which was in keeping with its claimed top speed of 240mph. Borrowing many of the mechanical components from the Jaguar XJ220, the GT90 featured a drag co-efficient of just 0.32; pretty much as aerodynamically efficient as it's possible to get with a car of this type. It was light too, thanks to an aluminium honeycomb monocoque with carbon-fibre panelling, for the optimum balance between strength and lightness. Putting the power down were 19-inch wheels at each corner, with rear-wheel drive.

Statistics

Type of vehicle	**Supercar**
Year	**1995**
Country of origin	**USA**
Length	**4470mm**
Width	**1963mm**
Height	**1140mm**
Engine size	**5927cc**
Engine type	**Mid-mounted quad-turbo petrol V12**
Max power	**720bhp**
Max speed	**235mph**
Number of seats	**2**
Special features	**A V12 with four turbochargers, plus that crazy angular design**
Extreme rating	**9**

Freddy's Revenge
Dragster

Freddy's Revenge
Dragster

When Dante Giacosa set out in the 1930s to design the Fiat Topolino, a small family car to mobilise Italy's masses, he probably didn't think there'd be a 1400bhp replica racing around 70 years later – but there is. Capable of more than 200mph, and able to sprint from standstill to 190mph in just 7.1 seconds, Freddy's Revenge isn't your average 1930s economy car. Indeed, at full chat it burns fuel at the rate of 16 gallons per mile, so there's nothing economical about it. The car was even more of a replica after its first run on the drag strip in 2005, when it hit the concrete barriers at high speed and destroyed itself. The team didn't give in though; it was up and running again in just two months, developed even further with the aim of hitting 200mph in under seven seconds.

Type of vehicle	**Nostalgia fuel altered dragster**
Year	**1938/2005**
Country of origin	**UK**
Length	**N/A**
Width	**N/A**
Height	**N/A**
Engine size	**8538cc**
Engine type	**Front-mounted supercharged petrol V8**
Max power	**1400bhp**
Max speed	**200mph+**
Number of seats	**1**
Special features	**Eye-popping performance**
Extreme rating	**10**

Pictures courtesy of www.freddysrevenge.co.uk

IFR Aspid

IFR
Aspid

You certainly wouldn't buy it for its looks, but if eye-watering acceleration is your thing, you could do a lot worse than buy an IFR Aspid. Five years in the making, the Aspid features a 2-litre Honda-sourced VTEC engine, supercharged to give an astonishing 400bhp. That's enough to give 0–62mph in just 2.8 seconds, although a cheaper Supersport edition packs a mere 270bhp, giving a 0–62mph time of 3.9 seconds. The key to such performance is a hyper-light construction, which is why the suspension and chassis are made of aluminium while the body tub is built of carbon fibre; the car's dry weight is just 700kg. Despite the low weight, the cars aren't stripped-out specials, as standard kit includes climate control, a fixed roof and a touch screen for controlling the car's major functions.

Statistics

Type of vehicle	**Roadster**
Year	**2008**
Country of origin	**Spain**
Length	**3750mm**
Width	**1870mm**
Height	**1160mm**
Engine size	**1997cc**
Engine type	**Supercharged four-cylinder petrol**
Max power	**400bhp**
Max speed	**155mph**
Number of seats	**2**
Special features	**Mind-blowing acceleration and a chronically ugly design**
Extreme rating	**7**

Irmscher
Inspiro

Irmscher
Inspiro

It was never going to win any beauty prizes, but the Irmscher Inspiro could certainly claim to offer striking (if somewhat challenging) looks. Better known for its work tuning the products of Opel, Irmscher decided to create its own two-seater roadster for the 2002 Geneva motor show, powered by an Opel Omega-sourced 3-litre V6, putting out 225bhp. So endowed, the car was capable of sprinting from 0 to 62mph in just 5.8 seconds, thanks to a kerb weight of just 780kg. That power was channelled to the rear wheels via a five-speed manual gearbox and limited-slip differential. At each corner there was a 19-inch alloy wheel, while braking was provided by four-pot callipers gripping ventilated discs. When the car was introduced, no mention was made of the possibility of production; thankfully it didn't happen.

Statistics

Type of vehicle	**Roadster**
Year	**2002**
Country of origin	**Germany**
Length	**4100mm**
Width	**1820mm**
Height	**1275mm**
Engine size	**2962cc**
Engine type	**Front-mounted V6 petrol**
Max power	**225bhp**
Max speed	**149mph**
Number of seats	**2**
Special features	**Strong performance and, er, striking looks. Okay – so it was hideously ugly**
Extreme rating	**7**

Jeep
Treo

Jeep
Treo

Saving the planet and off roading may appear to be at opposite ends of the environmental spectrum, but that didn't stop Jeep from creating this eco-friendly 4x4 to put the green into green laning. Intended to be a glimpse into the future, the Treo was built on a platform that could carry a zero-emission fuel cell or some other form of high-tech propulsion. Inside there was space for two in the front, while the rear seat could fold flat for storage of luggage. Alternatively, the front wheels from the supplied mountain bikes could be removed and mounted in the rear of the interior, while still allowing a third passenger to ride along. With drive-by-wire for all major functions and a pair of electric motors to provide drive to all four corners, the Treo could justifiably claim to be a proper Jeep while also showing the way forward in terms of eco friendliness. Let's hope that vision becomes a reality.

Statistics

Type of vehicle	Eco off-roader
Year	2003
Country of origin	USA
Length	3235mm
Width	1680mm
Height	1585mm
Engine size	N/A
Engine type	Fuel cell
Max power	N/A
Max speed	N/A
Number of seats	3
Special features	2+1 seating, fuel cell propulsion
Extreme rating	7

Lotus
2-Eleven

Lotus
2-Eleven

Lotus is no stranger to extreme cars, but the 2-Eleven must rank as the most far-out machine ever to come from the Hethel company – wackier even than the limited-run 340R. Indeed, the 340R was seen as something of a missed opportunity as it was styling-led; the 2-Eleven aims to change that, with a chassis that can live up to the exterior design. Based on the platform of a Mk1 Elise, the 2-Eleven packs a supercharged Toyota-sourced 1.8-litre engine, and while the car isn't road-legal as it comes out of the factory, it is possible to make a few tweaks to register it for the road. For those who insist on using their 2-Eleven on the public road, there's also a normally aspirated edition; capable of despatching the 0–100mph sprint in just 13.3 seconds, that's plenty quick enough for most.

Statistics

Type of vehicle	Track car for the road
Year	2007
Country of origin	England
Length	3822mm
Width	1735mm
Height	1112mm
Engine size	1796cc
Engine type	Mid-mounted supercharged four-cylinder petrol
Max power	252bhp
Max speed	150mph
Number of seats	2
Special features	Track-focused handling, astonishing performance
Extreme rating	7

Mansory
Bel Air

Mansory
Bel Air

There was a time when Rolls-Royce produced ultra-exclusive cars, but nowadays the company's products are just a little bit too common for some. Thankfully, there will always be companies on hand to ensure that if all your neighbours have got a Phantom Drophead Coupé just like yours, you can have a retrim and a fresh set of wheels to make it look that bit different. Named after the fashionable Los Angeles district, the Bel Air was fitted with polished 22-inch spoked alloy wheels, behind which sat a specially designed Brembo braking system, complete with 412mm diameter discs at the front. Some would question how tasteful Mansory's modifications are, and it's pretty doubtful that Rolls-Royce would have anything positive to say about them – but you can't deny the company's cars stand out from the crowd.

Statistics

Type of vehicle	Four-seater convertible
Year	2007
Country of origin	England/Germany
Length	5609mm
Width	1987mm
Height	1581mm
Engine size	6749cc
Engine type	Front-mounted petrol V12
Max power	453bhp
Max speed	149mph
Number of seats	4
Special features	Utterly tasteless inside and out; Rolls and Royce would be spinning in their graves
Extreme rating	6

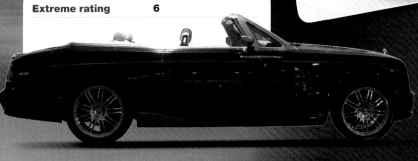

Mazda
RX-7 drift car

K827
PHW

Mazda
RX-7 drift car

The third-generation RX-7 has long been a tuner's favourite, with lairy bodywork, mental paint schemes and insane power levels par for the course. Indeed, compared to some of the examples out there, this 1993 drift car looks relatively tame. However, while there's no pearlescent paint job, you'll find plenty of bodywork mods – but it's under the skin where the real treats lie in store. The rotary engine has been blown to give a massive 550bhp, while to rein the car in a very tasty set of brakes have been fitted – they're the same as those you'd normally see on a Ferrari F40. To accommodate those extra-wide wheels the bodywork has had to be widened by 50mm, while the beetle-wing doors provide the finishing touch for when the car is on display.

Statistics

Type of vehicle	**Drift car**
Year	**1993**
Country of origin	**Japan/UK**
Length	**4282mm**
Width	**1750mm**
Height	**1229mm**
Engine size	**1.3 litres**
Engine type	**Front-mounted turbo petrol rotary**
Max power	**550bhp**
Max speed	**180mph**
Number of seats	**4**
Special features	**Insane power from a relatively small rotary engine, crazy bodywork**
Extreme rating	**8**

Thanks to www.severnside-imports.co.uk

Mazda
Taiki

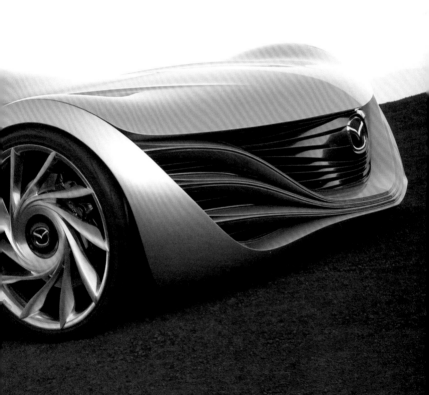

Mazda
Taiki

One of many concepts that followed Mazda's Nagare (or 'Flow' in English) design theme, the Taiki represented an alternative view of how an energy-efficient two-seater sportscar could look in the future. The brief for the car was to come up with a design that "visually expresses the flow of air inspired by the image of a pair of hagoramo floating down from the sky". You could be forgiven for being unfamiliar with the hagoramo; they're the flowing robes that enabled a celestial maiden to fly in Japanese legend. While the overall design was eye-catching, so too were the details such as the wheel design that was inspired by turbine blades. However, equally intriguing was an interior that was black on the driver's side to help with concentration, but white on the passenger's side in a bid to ease relaxation.

Statistics

Type of vehicle	**Sportscar**
Year	**2007**
Country of origin	**Japan**
Length	**4620mm**
Width	**1950mm**
Height	**1240mm**
Engine size	**N/A**
Engine type	**Rotary petrol engine**
Max power	**N/A**
Max speed	**N/A**
Number of seats	**2**
Special features	**A drag coefficient of just 0.25, plus gorgeous curves everywhere**
Extreme rating	**8**

Mercedes
F400 Carving

Mercedes
F400 Carving

You can bet it's going to be a long time yet before some of the
key technologies showcased in the F400 Carving will be seen
in a mainstream production car, even though the concept
was shown as far back as 2001. Items such as braking and
steering by wire aren't likely to be legalised any time soon,
but it's the cost of implementation that'll hold back many
of the features. The key one is a crazy suspension system,
which allowed the front wheels to lean into a bend to optimise
the available grip, adjusting the camber by up to 20 degrees
in either direction. It's this facility that gave the car its name;
carving is a skiing technique in which the skier leans into the
bend to achieve the ultimate in cornering power.

Statistics

Type of vehicle	Sportscar
Year	2001
Country of origin	Germany
Length	3979mm
Width	1890mm
Height	1150mm
Engine size	3201cc
Engine type	Front-mounted supercharged petrol V6
Max power	350bhp
Max speed	150mph
Number of seats	2
Special features	Steering and braking by wire, plus variable-camber suspension
Extreme rating	9

Monstrous
Monster truck

Take one 1997 Ford F150 pick-up truck then tweak it a bit (well, quite a lot in fact), and you'll end up with the monster you see here, aptly called Monstrous. The twin brother of Bigfoot 17, Monstrous is the European edition of an American icon that's been doing the rounds since 1979, racing and driving over cars to thrill crowds across the US. Although the gear ratios usually mean Monstrous isn't especially fast, with the right transmission fitted the thing can achieve 80mph – and when you think the truck sits on 66-inch tyres and has rear-wheel steering, that's a pretty frightening prospect! However, such driving is restricted to closed circuits, because with a width of around 12 feet, Monstrous is too wide to be driven on public roads.

Statistics

Type of vehicle	**Monster truck**
Year	**2003**
Country of origin	**UK**
Length	**5791mm**
Width	**3962mm**
Height	**3353mm**
Engine size	**9.2 litres**
Engine type	**Supercharged V8**
Max power	**1978bhp**
Max speed	**75mph**
Number of seats	**1**
Special features	**66-inch tyres, can float on water, can drive over anything**
Extreme rating	**9**

Pictures courtesy of www.monstermania.eu

Nick Gale Customs
Rosso Corsa

Nick Gale Customs
Rosso Corsa

It takes something pretty special to turn the eye of Ferrari supremo Jean Todt, but that's exactly what Nick Gale's Harley-Davidson-based Rosso Corsa did – so much so that Todt bought the machine to display in the Ferrari museum in Modena. Gale had already swept the board with his Memphis Belle custom bike, which had won all the European HOG custom trophies going. Rosso Corsa was created to carry on where Memphis Belle left off; a task it accomplished with ease, taking trophies galore throughout the 2005 season. The departure of the bike to Modena meant something fresh had to be created though, which is why Nick Gale set about creating Little Miss Dynamite – something that's visually less extreme, and more of a racer than a cruiser.

Type of vehicle	Custom motorcycle
Year	2005
Country of origin	UK
Length	Approx 2800mm
Width	Approx 920mm
Height	Approx 1170mm
Engine size	1340cc
Engine type	Mid-mounted petrol V-twin
Max power	N/A
Max speed	N/A
Number of seats	1
Special features	A 360mm wide rear tyre
Extreme rating	8

Pictures courtesy of
www.nickgalecustoms.co.uk

Nissan
Silvia Drift Car

Nissan
Silvia Drift Car

To see a top-notch drifter in action is to witness driving at its most skilled. However, it's not just the driver that needs to be good; the car needs to be special too – and you'll have to look hard to find a drift car more special than this. While a decent drift car needs at least 350bhp, the blown straight-six in this monster can develop a massive 572bhp. Costing £100,000 to build over an 18-month period, the car was built with the help of Garage-D Federal Tyres, japaneseusedcars.com and driftworks.com, the biggest job entailing moving the engine and gearbox back 32cm, to even out the weight distribution between the axles. The car is now claimed to be about as highly developed as a drift car can be – but no doubt that's only until somebody does something even crazier.

Statistics

Type of vehicle	**Drift car**
Year	**2008**
Country of origin	**Japan/UK**
Length	**4445mm**
Width	**1695mm**
Height	**1265mm**
Engine size	**3 litres**
Engine type	**Front-mounted turbocharged petrol straight-six**
Max power	**572bhp**
Max speed	**N/A**
Number of seats	**2**
Special features	**Capable of creating more black smoke than a burning oil tanker**
Extreme rating	**7**

Thanks to www.driftworks.com

Nissan
Urge

Nissan Urge

The Urge was born from an online survey that Nissan conducted into the buying habits of young Americans, which concluded that performance and technology were their key requirements. Something that was fun to drive was needed, but it had to incorporate such gadgets as a mobile phone, MP3 player and games console – while also being affordable. It was the games console that was foremost in the designers' minds, with several of the styling cues revolving around this. With a sense of adventure being a part of the gamer's make up, the Urge was intended to be a bit off-the-wall while also being real-world enough to be usable as an everyday driver. Nissan didn't specify what engine was fitted, but it claimed the powerplant would be a high-revving small-displacement unit, mounted at the front and driving the rear wheels.

Statistics

Type of vehicle	Sportscar
Year	2006
Country of origin	Japan
Length	3979mm
Width	1824mm
Height	1260mm
Engine size	N/A
Engine type	Front-mounted petrol four-cylinder
Max power	Approx 140bhp
Max speed	Approx 140mph
Number of seats	2
Special features	See-through bodywork, exposed chassis frame, high gadget count
Extreme rating	8

Peugeot
20Cup

Peugeot
20Cup

Almost a century earlier, Morgan had introduced the idea of a three-wheeled sportscar – an idea that Peugeot refined considerably with its 20Cup of 2005. The idea is simple: by simplifying the car to the max, weight can be reduced for maximum agility and performance. Whether or not losing a wheel really helps cornering ability is open to debate, but with less than 500kg to haul, the turbocharged petrol engine didn't have to work too hard to put a grin on the driver's face. That engine was the same unit that BMW fitted to its second-generation Mini, as it was developed in conjunction with Peugeot. Whereas most sportscars offer steering at the front and drive to the rear, the 20Cup reversed this, while also reducing the centre of gravity to the max, to ensure truly superb handling.

Statistics

Type of vehicle	Roadster
Year	2005
Country of origin	France
Length	3630mm
Width	1770mm
Height	2310mm
Engine size	1.6-litre
Engine type	Front-mounted turbocharged petrol four-cylinder
Max power	168bhp
Max speed	Approx 140mph
Number of seats	2
Special features	Great looks and a missing wheel, plus performance galore
Extreme rating	8

Peugeot
Moovie

Peugeot
Moovie

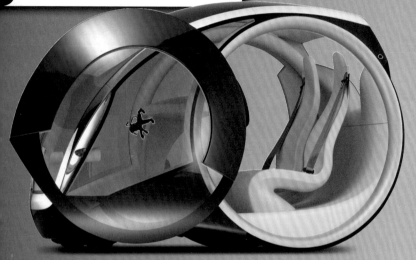

A non-running prototype, the Moovie concept was one of the weirdest motoring creations ever. The concept was the result of a global design competition set up by Peugeot, the winner being honoured with a full-scale model to be displayed at a major international motor show. In the case of the Moovie, the designer was 23-year old André Costa, with his design being unveiled at the 2005 Frankfurt motor show. The Moovie was full of neat touches, such as circular doors which housed the rear wheels, plus front wheels which were effectively large castors, for the ultimate in manouevrability. The cutting-edge design continued inside, with a light, airy cabin surrounded by glass and capable of providing seating for two. There wasn't much luggage space though and not much room for any form of motive power – but maybe one day...

Statistics

Type of vehicle	City car
Year	2005
Country of origin	France
Length	2330mm
Width	1800mm
Height	1540mm
Engine size	N/A
Engine type	Electric
Max power	N/A
Max speed	N/A
Number of seats	2
Special features	One of the craziest and least practical car designs ever conceived
Extreme rating	10

Pininfarina
Birdcage

Pininfarina
Birdcage

Maserati has a glorious heritage, yet it has always been seen as the poor relation to Ferrari. So, to celebrate its 75th birthday, Pininfarina decided to do an update of a Maserati milestone, creating a Birdcage for the 21st century – a homage to an icon that was originally born 45 years earlier. The car had to be an ultimate – something that would stop the Geneva motor show when it was unveiled. That meant a show-stopping design; less than 43 inches tall at its highest point, the Birdcage's low height was accentuated by massive wheels which were 20 inches across at the front and 22 inches at the back. There were some pretty radical mechanicals too; what better than those which normally lived under the ultra-exclusive Maserati MC12, itself based on the Ferrari Enzo? Production was never suggested; if it had been, the car would have been guaranteed to sell out.

Statistics

Type of vehicle	**Supercar**
Year	**2005**
Country of origin	**Italy**
Length	**4656mm**
Width	**2020mm**
Height	**1090mm**
Engine size	**5998cc**
Engine type	**Mid-mounted V12 petrol**
Max power	**700bhp**
Max speed	**200mph+**
Number of seats	**2**
Special features	**LED lighting throughout, a head-up display for the driver, plus Maserati MC12 power.**
Extreme rating	**9**

Renault
Racoon

Renault
Racoon

Renault described is as a 'freedom car of tomorrow' when it was unveiled, but little did the company know that when the Racoon debuted in 1993, the words 'freedom' and 'car' would soon become one of the least politically correct phrases known to man. Still, that didn't stop the French company from dreaming of the day when an amphibious 4x4 would be snapped up by eager buyers, keen to traverse deserts. With a cabin inspired by a helicopter's bubble cockpit, four legs sprouted from the Racoon's bodyshell, to which were attached the wheels. These legs could be adjusted to give anywhere 300mm and 500mm of ground clearance. Oddly enough, we're still waiting for the production version.

Statistics

Type of vehicle	Amphibious SUV
Year	1993
Country of origin	France
Length	N/A
Width	N/A
Height	N/A
Engine size	2963cc
Engine type	Rear-mounted twin-turbo petrol V6
Max power	262bhp
Max speed	97mph
Number of seats	3
Special features	Amphibious, an untrasonic sensor that vapourises water as it hits the windscreen
Extreme rating	10

Rinspeed
Senso

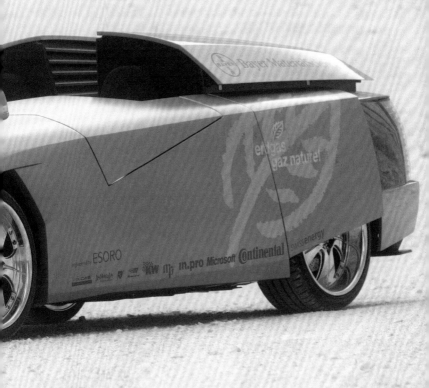

Rinspeed
Senso

Another bonkers idea from Frank Rinderknecht's Swiss company, the Senso was a car which detected its driver's biometric data and adjusted various elements to suit. So depending on the driver's pulse, blood pressure and alertness, the Senso could alter the colour of the interior lighting, play different types of music within the cabin and even emit different fragrances. Vents were scattered around the cabin; they emitted various scents from citrus to vanilla depending on the driver's mood. As if this wasn't mad enough, the Senso was also environmentally friendly, as it ran on natural gas. Or at least it was probably as environmentally friendly as it's possible to be with a Porsche Boxster 3.2-litre flat-six mounted in the middle. Also, for strength and lightness, the bodywork was made of plastic composites – but they could all be recycled.

Statistics

Type of vehicle	**Sportscar**
Year	**2005**
Country of origin	**Switzerland**
Length	**4475mm**
Width	**1820mm**
Height	**1200mm**
Engine size	**3179cc**
Engine type	**Mid-mounted petrol flat-six**
Max power	**250bhp**
Max speed	**155mph**
Number of seats	**2**
Special features	**Variable exterior colours, plus variable interior smells**
Extreme rating	**9**

Rinspeed
sQuba

Rinspeed
sQuba

You can always count on Rinspeed to come up with something
completely insane at the Geneva motor show each spring. The
company's 2008 effort was this Lotus Elise that was capable of
being driven underwater, inspired by James Bond's Lotus Esprit in
The Spy Who Loved Me. Powered by three electric motors installed
where the petrol engine normally lives, one provides propulsion on
land, while the other two drive the screws for underwater motoring.
They're supported by two powerful Seabob jet drives in the front,
which 'breathe' through rotating louvres to propel the car at up to
2mph under water or 4mph when on the surface. Most incredibly
though, using a series of lasers, the sQuba is capable of driving
itself on land without any human intervention. Scary stuff…

Statistics

Type of vehicle	**Amphibious sportscar**
Year	**2008**
Country of origin	**Switzerland**
Length	**3785mm**
Width	**1940mm**
Height	**1117mm**
Engine size	**Electric**
Engine type	**Electric moor**
Max power	**54Kw (72bhp)**
Max speed	**75mph**
Number of seats	**2**
Special features	**It can drive on or under water, plus it's an electric Lotus Elise. It can also drive itself.**
Extreme rating	**10**

Smart
Crossblade

Smart
Crossblade

One of the few genuine production cars here, the Smart Crossblade was also one of the craziest and least practical machines ever offered in significant numbers. When it was first shown at the 2001 Geneva motor show, few reckoned Smart would really go through with putting the car into production – but that's just what it did. However, it was never going to be a big seller, and considering the car could carry just two people at no more than 85mph, with little in the way of creature comforts, the Crossblade was far too costly at around £16,000. Still, it could offer a driving experience somewhere between a Caterham Seven and a fairground ride, and thanks to hose-down neoprene interior trim, it didn't matter that there was no form of protection from the elements.

Statistics

Type of vehicle	Urban roadster
Year	2002
Country of origin	Germany
Length	2622mm
Width	1618mm
Height	1508mm
Engine size	599cc
Engine type	Rear-mounted turbocharged petrol three-cylinder
Max power	70bhp
Max speed	85mph
Number of seats	2
Special features	No weather equipment whatsoever, wash-down interior
Extreme rating	8

Suzuki
PIXY and SSC

Suzuki
PIXY and SSC

For those of us who can't bear to make even the shortest of journeys on foot, Suzuki has come up with personal transport to get you to and from your personal transport. That's right; the Suzuki Shared Coach is a transporter for a pair of PIXY single-person buggies, so you never have to walk anywhere again – although what happens when a set of stairs is encountered hasn't been disclosed. The idea is that you whizz about in your PIXY at a very local level, but if you're travelling further afield, up to two people can put their PIXYs onto the SSC, to complete the longer journey. The SSC is symmetrical in both planes, with each end featuring a top-hinged door, allowing the PIXY to be driven in from either direction. Not at all mad...

Statistics

Type of vehicle	**Urban runabout**
Year	**2008**
Country of origin	**Japan**
Length	**Approx 2500mm**
Width	**Approx 1300mm**
Height	**Approx 1800mm**
Engine size	**N/A**
Engine type	**Electric motor**
Max power	**N/A**
Max speed	**N/A**
Number of seats	**Up to 2**
Special features	**Completely barking mad and a couch potato's dream**
Extreme rating	**8**

Talon
Quad

Talon
Quad

Quads tend to look like four-wheeled motorbikes, but in the case of the Talon the design has more in common with a fairground dodgem than a go-anywhere all-terrain vehicle. Accepting that an increasing number of people are choosing to use a quad bike as everyday short-distance transport, Dale Aurich decided to come up with something more stylish than the typical design. He came up with the Talon, powered by a Kawasaki four-stroke motorbike engine and offering eye-catching looks from every angle. Everything is designed for maximum visual effect, from the integrated headlamps to the smart alloy wheels, while those who want something even more distinctive can specify split-rim alloys or a custom paint job. But with just six inches of ground clearance, this isn't a vehicle for tackling the rough stuff.

Statistics

Type of vehicle	Quad
Year	2008
Country of origin	USA
Length	2718mm
Width	1270mm
Height	1092mm
Engine size	697cc
Engine type	Petrol V-twin
Max power	45bhp
Max speed	Approx 75mph
Number of seats	1
Special features	A genuinely stylish design – for a quad
Extreme rating	6

Tilly 3
Top Fuel Motorbike

Tilly 3
Top Fuel Motorbike

Drag racing a car is one thing, but doing it on a bike is something else altogether – your nerves need to be made of far tougher stuff than steel. While there are even crazier bikes than this that take part in drag racing, none look as fabulous as this beautifully streamlined creation, put together by UK-based Les Harris. One of just three streamliners built, Tilly 3 features a one-off hand-built steel-tube frame, around which is wrapped a carbon-fibre fairing to reduce drag – making the bike much quicker in the process. Despite the effectiveness of the ultra-slippery bodywork, this is one of only two such machines still raced, the other being in Australia. It doesn't end here though; the next step is a 185bhp machine, using the mechanicals from a snowmobile!

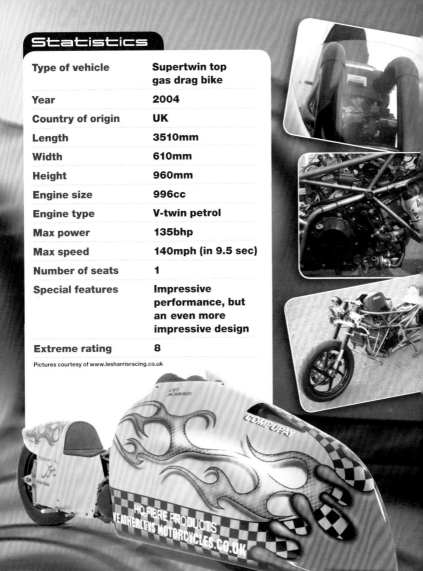

Statistics

Type of vehicle	Supertwin top gas drag bike
Year	2004
Country of origin	UK
Length	3510mm
Width	610mm
Height	960mm
Engine size	996cc
Engine type	V-twin petrol
Max power	135bhp
Max speed	140mph (in 9.5 sec)
Number of seats	1
Special features	Impressive performance, but an even more impressive design
Extreme rating	8

Pictures courtesy of www.lesharrisracing.co.uk

Toyota
MTRC

Toyota
MTRC

Featured in the Gran Turismo 4 video game, the Toyota MTRC offered a true glimpse into the future, with a whole range of technologies that will probably never reach fruition. The key one of these was a set of tyres which could stiffen or soften to suit the prevailing road conditions. The car's occupants also wore special helmets which featured head-up displays, capable of displaying information about upcoming road conditions and the state of the tyres. Meanwhile, the suspension was fully adjustable for both height and stiffness, everything being taken care of automatically by the car depending on how hard it was being driven. Motive power was provided by a fuel cell, which supplied energy to electric motors mounted in each wheel; this really was an exercise in automotive escapism.

Statistics

Type of vehicle	**Sportscar**
Year	**2004**
Country of origin	**Japan**
Length	**4060mm**
Width	**1930mm**
Height	**1330mm**
Engine size	**N/A**
Engine type	**Fuel cell**
Max power	**N/A**
Max speed	**N/A**
Number of seats	**2**
Special features	**Intelligent tyres, adjustable ride height, head-up displays**
Extreme rating	**10**

Venturi
Astrolab

Venturi
Astrolab

You can always rely on Venturi to come up with something off the wall; the French company is incapable of coming up with a boring concept or design. Originally known for its supercars, the company set off in a fresh direction in the 21st century, starting with the Lotus Elise-like electric Fétish that debuted in concept form in 2002. One of the follow up models included the Astrolab, which is covered in solar panels so its batteries can be recharged while in motion. The entire upper surface of the ultra-light carbon-fibre body tub is covered in solar cells which don't need direct sunlight to charge the batteries. With aerodynamics more like those of an aircraft, an overall mass of just 280kg, and tyres that are just 130mm across to reduce the rolling resistance to a minimum, Venturi has pulled out all the stops to create the most energy-efficient transport possible.

Type of vehicle	Electric quadricycle
Year	2006
Country of origin	France
Length	3800mm
Width	1840mm
Height	1200mm
Engine size	N/A
Engine type	Asynchronous electric motor
Max power	21bhp
Max speed	75mph
Number of seats	2
Special features	Solar powered, tandem seats, open wheels
Extreme rating	10

VW
GX3

VW
GX3

Would you believe that the same company which builds millions of Golfs and Polos every year is capable of churning out something as funky and exciting as this? That's right, the company with obsessive attention to detail occasionally indulges in a bit of fun, and believe it or not, the GX3 was seriously considered for production. Dreamed up by VW's Californian Design Centre, the GX3 wasn't a car with a wheel missing – it was a motorbike with an extra wheel. Bizarrely, this was also VW's vision of the future of commuting; the company reckoned that by removing the roof and fitting just one wheel at the back instead of two, the daily drive to work would somehow become a dream journey. It was hoped the trike could be offered for $17,000, but the plug was pulled when VW got cold feet over potential safety issues and the ensuing lawsuits from US buyers.

Type of vehicle	Three-wheeled roadster
Year	2006
Country of origin	Germany
Length	3753mm
Width	1850mm
Height	1210mm
Engine size	1.6-litre
Engine type	Four-cylinder mid-mounted petrol
Max power	125bhp
Max speed	125mph
Number of seats	2
Special features	Three wheels, the ability to offer 0–62mph in 5.7 seconds with 46mpg potential
Extreme rating	9

Weber
Faster One

Weber
Faster One

Its maker calls it the Faster One, but a more apt name would be the Uglier One. Looking as though it was styled by a five-year old, the Weber certainly has presence. It also has a twin-supercharged 7-litre V8 engine in the middle, churning out a claimed 900 horses. As a result, the car is supposedly capable of topping 250mph – not that anyone has yet verified this of course. The car is claimed to be capable of such high speeds because of an ultra-light carbon-fibre bodyshell, while carbon-ceramic brakes ensure the Weber doesn't run out of stopping power in even the toughest of conditions. Optional equipment includes a multi-media system with internet access and TV, a data logger for track use while all cars are fitted with four fuel tanks to feed that thirsty V8.

Statistics

Type of vehicle	**Supercar**
Year	**2008**
Country of origin	**Switzerland**
Length	**4500mm**
Width	**2040mm**
Height	**1150mm**
Engine size	**7 litres**
Engine type	**Mid-mounted twin-supercharged petrol V8**
Max power	**900bhp**
Max speed	**250mph (claimed)**
Number of seats	**2**
Special features	**Unfeasibly ugly design, active aerodynamics**
Extreme rating	**8**

www.haynes.co.uk

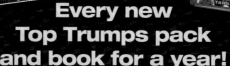